Crater
and
Tower

Crater
and
Tower

poems by
Cheryl J. Fish

SHANTI ARTS PUBLISHING
BRUNSWICK, MAINE

Crater and Tower (expanded edition)

Published by Shanti Arts LLC, 193 Hillside Road,
Brunswick, Maine 04011; shantiarts.com
First published by Duck Lake Books, 2020

Designed by Shanti Arts Designs

Cover images—(1) New York skyline silhouette with Twin
Towers at sunset, 09.11.2001, American Patriot Day banner,
NYC World Trade Center, hamara / 525885765 / stock.
adobe.com; (2) Eruption column from May 18, 1980 Mount
St. Helens, Photograph by Austin Post, Volcano Hazards
Program, United States Geological Survey. Public domain.

Interior images (page 2)—(1) Mt. St. Helens before the
eruption, Photograph by Harry Glicken, Geology and
Ecology of National Parks, United States Geological
Survey. Public domain; (2) World Trade Center,
Photograph by Tom Harpel, 1999. Wikimedia Commons,
Creative Commons Attribution 2.0 Generic license.

Printed in the United States of America

ISBN: 978-1-962082-77-8 (softcover)

Library of Congress Control Number: 2025940108

CONTENTS

ROCK THAT VORTEX

ASH FOR CASH

OFF-SIDE

POST-TRAUMATIC POSTS

ACKNOWLEDGMENTS

Thank you, Christine Cote, for publishing this expanded edition of *Crater and Tower* with Shanti Arts. During the first year of the COVID pandemic, shortly after this book first appeared, Duck Lake Books shut down and the collection went out of print. I would like to thank Charles Goodrich and the Spring Creek Project at Oregon State University for providing a writer-in-residence fellowship to attend the Pulse Gathering of Scientists at Mount St. Helens Volcanic National Monument where a number of these poems were first conceived. Sincere appreciation to the librarians and staff at the Oregon Historical Society, the Washington State Archives in Olympia, and the Special Collections of the University of Washington Library for help with print and multimedia items that inspired some of the poems. Thanks to the Office of Academic Affairs at Borough of Manhattan Community College, City University of New York, and the PSC/CUNY Research Foundation, for grants enabling travel to collections that held manuscripts, electronic and print materials, and objects that inspired some of these poems. Grateful appreciation to Christine Colarsurdo, Elaine Equi, Sri Lal, Joel Lewis, Elinor Mattern, Kimo Reder, Michelle M. Tokarczyk, and Lee Upton for reading and providing feedback on versions of the poems or the manuscript. Also, thanks to my current poetry group, Michelle M. Tokarczyk, Eileen P. Kennedy, and Ellen Rittberg for feedback on drafts of the poems added to this edition.

•

The author would like to acknowledge the editors of the following journals and anthologies for publishing these poems, sometimes in different versions:

Big City Review: "Night Light"

Gyroscope Review (2016): "Off-Side"

Hanging Loose (2018): "Ash for Cash" and "Harry Truman of St. Helens Lodge"

ISLE: Interdisciplinary Studies in Literature and Environment (Spring 2019): "Dear Governor Ray"; "Dust Lady Dies of Cancer"; and "Metallic Thud"

Kudzu House Quarterly (2015): "Volcano Moves"

Lalitamba: A Journal of International Writings for Liberation (2019): "Flexible Bark"

Maintenant: A Journal of Contemporary Dada Writing (2019): "Simon Says"

Mom Egg Review (2021): "I Never Had a Daughter" and "Blanks (Iceland 5)"

Newtown Literary Review (2017): "Losses We Cover"; "Lost Friends"; and "Mom Out of the Bleachers"

NOW: Online Magazine of Hobart Festival of Women Writers (2024): "Abecedarian: She Cries"

Poems from the Wellspring (2019): "Harry Truman of St. Helens Lodge""

Reed Magazine (2016): "Hula-Hoop Mojo"

Talisman: A Journal of Contemporary Poetry and Poetics (2019): "Joe's Pizza Heartbreak Slice" and "Playing Style"

Terrain.org: A Journal of Built and Natural Environment (2013): "Blind Spot" and "Volcanic/Panic" (text and audio)

Tribeca Poetry Review (2012): "Daycare Dads"

Volt: A Magazine of the Arts (2014): "Aerial"

•

"Sweep-Second Hand" appeared in the author's chapbook *My City Flies By* (E. G. Press, 1986).

"Aerial"; "Fundraiser for Hackensack River Keeper"; and "Yeti in Portland" appeared in the author's Belladonna Chaplet 171 (2014), *Make It Funny, Make It Last.*

•

Some poems were inspired by documents in these collections:

Betty Lou Rogers, Oral memoir, SR 1527, Oregon Historical Society Research Library

William R. Halladay, File 5013-002, Special Collections, University of Washington.

Dixie Lee Ray, Papers, Washington State Archives, Southwest Regional Branch, Olympia

PROLOGUE: A MULTI-VERSE

Trauma haunts and burrows. It is not like growing hair or nails, not automatic.

A group of writers and artists, thirty years post-eruption, spent a week at Mount St. Helens National Volcanic Monument where scientists record and share data on ecological change over time. They measure and document. But poets?

We are charged with perceiving "temporal dimensions…and after reflection, turning to our writing to provide insights scientists might ignore." Like Wordsworth's emotion reflected in tranquility? NO. There's blazing energy in the standing dead remains of old growth trees, the uncanny and invisible. Cowlitz and Yakama tribes leave traces, tales of former residents and lodgers, and the agency of trees, rock and tephra. Multiple voices register, creatures stir.

Imagination and indignation.
This collection: a multi-verse. Shimmering.

Mount St. Helens erupted on May 18, 1980, blowing off more than 1,000 feet from the mountain top. Giant landslides clogged rivers, a crater replaced a summit, debris avalanches moved chunks of mountainside. I witnessed the terrifying events of September 11, 2001, from a few blocks away as a resident and professor at a nearby community college, evacuating students, running to my two-year-old in a nearby daycare center. I even voted as it was primary day. Trauma's effect: movement inside dismay.

The charred and beautiful post-eruption landscapes, the idea of "succession" from scientists, geological events like toxic particles lodged in our bodies. Only later would I consider smoke and ash at both places, fragments of bone and rock, shock and death, the interplay between "natural" and "manmade" disasters, the forces of commerce and politics commodifying loss, failing to acknowledge certain forms. Vandana Shiva calls it "maldevelopment." Wonder. Paralysis. The absurd. How and when can we reconcile?

For the Cowlitz tribe, place is fluid, revealing their concept of reality. For poet Gary Snyder, Mount St. Helens evoked his experience hiking on the peak shortly after the U.S. dropped the bomb on Hiroshima, and then again after the 1980 eruption. From the distance of a continent and nine years, with that crater in my periphery, I process the events of 9-11 in my neighborhood, its unfolding aftermath. At sites Anna Storm calls post-industrial landscape scars, what are our priorities? Who speaks? Who has power? What choices do we make? How are we living in place? These poems attempt to conjure many perspectives and voices, from Bigfoot to "dust lady."

With the added reflection of four years since writing this, disasters, war, and chaos reign supreme near and far threatening our planet. In the face of ongoing calamities, we must not forget the events of 9/11/01 and the illnesses that resulted from exposure magnifying as time passes. The responses by leaders to that dreadful day and its aftermath often fell short. And the largest volcanic eruption in North America in the twentieth century offers us not only a glimpse of geological cosmologies and the earth's forces repeating through time, but our temporal experience of their power.

This expanded collection begins with two new poems reflecting on changes since the original *Crater and Tower* appeared in 2020.

ABECEDARIAN: TWENTY-THREE YEARS SINCE 9/11

All those years ago, already twenty-three. We await the
Bright memorial, night sky filled with Tower beams.
Community kept us together. Then came
Disaster drills and protocols, homeland security to
Elicit reduced risk, anticipate threats.
Fresh pandemic excavations in recent years, desertion, and fear.
Glistening Freedom Tower appeared with its underground malls.
Honors for some, fresh horror for others.
Incarnations of loss and gain. Lawyers urging
Justice on Facebook and TV. File claims!
Kick up dates and witnesses that prove you were there.
Liquidate trauma into compensation, survivor's
Mental health fissures, illnesses, unexamined talismans.
No stopping hawkers hawking souvenir picture books
    of the attack
On the plaza with a beer garden and hipster food trucks.
Pretend this never happened.
Quietly summon unexplainable sorrow.
Rest in restlessness, time may desensitize jumpy
Sensations. Young folks have no idea what happened on 9/11.
Terrorism, not experienced first-hand or second, but
    through images.
Undimmed, ongoing smoke and toxins remain eternal.
Violence is as violence does.
What might have accumulated in our cells?
X-rays, storyboards of lost emissions.
Your city, a gorgon, a gyroscope.
Zinnias adapt. Pink and yellow blossoms.
Aftermaths blooming eternally.

SLUMBERING

1.

Could a rural community of farmers and loggers,
of fishing and mountaineering, stay away from
A red zone of unstable dead trees, 80 billion gallons of
Muddy water upstream? Mount St. Helens spewed three
Empire-State-buildings worth of rock and ash
The equivalent of 50 million tons of TNT.
They called it a "slumbering princess."

The Cowlitz people know the mountain
as Sa Kw and Lawetlat'la.
Meaning "the smoker," and "where things happen."
Dispossessed, flow rises. They cannot rest.

2.

Could a city absorb fire in a pit where ashes broil?
Firefighters toiled for weeks, residents
Told it's safe to return home.
Terror spurs fear, desire for revenge. A void in the
topos. Planes crashed into towers, metal on metal.
Technological prowess, testosterone.
We were asleep.
"Just breathe" advised the
brochure. A "modest" excess of cancer
found among firefighters.
Now more than twenty years later, cancer appears often.
One-third of adults surveyed by the WTC Registry
report unmet mental health care needs
among 10-to-11-year-olds after 2001.

3.

In 2024, some youths have never heard of 9/11. In the midst
    of a pandemic,
a heating planet, in the wake of hurricanes, wars, artificial
    intelligence,
we slumber while awake.
Since February, 2024, Mount St. Helens rumbled with 350
    earthquakes
too small to be felt at the surface. In April, 2024, New York City
experienced an earthquake.
When my building shook, I envisioned planes. Collisions.
    More lost souls.

ONE

ROCK THAT VORTEX

"What can a volcano tell us about how to live?"

—Charles Goodrich

HULA-HOOP MOJO

Thirty years after Mount St. Helens
spoke with a maddening clarity
      I picked up a hula hoop near the shower trailers

      left by some child who forgot to pack it.
    I could swirl the hoop that morning, endlessly
It encircled me, a gravity polka
        Hips and lips and holes.

East to west, low to high
          I kept it spinning, it spun me.
Mountains have no apparent rhythms
     Like apparitions and lost souls.

Unsuspected hoopla can't be ruled out.

As a young girl I had known the joys of batons and hoops
     (but not since)
      twisting wrist, undulating tummy
Throwing them high for all to see
     you have to look at me.

Now with no one watching but birds
        And sullen peaks
      my hips rocked that vortex   plastic centrifugal force
        a lifeline.   Saturn's rings, kamikaze locomotive
near the volcano's
     geothermal underbelly.

Botched terrain in quiet glow of July.

    Surrounded by old growth forest

fir trees and mosses, girth of elephants' ears.

      Purple lupine and fanning ferns.

FLEXIBLE BARK

after evacuation
after afternoon
where are we?
who are they?

some could not run
some fell from buildings
some made it into boats

the wrong ones said go home

do images disappear?
who recalls landfill from before towers?
sand dunes where artists like Laurie Anderson performed.
who builds buildings, and who demolishes them?
who are the artful and who lack vision?

who desires revenge?
who follows orders?

The Lenape built dwellings of flexible bark
on this island
before it bore the weight of iron and steel.
Smoke escaped from cooking fires
in their dome roofs covered with bark.

Who thinks of them?

Oh Spirits within the realm
        Where do we think we plan to run?

THE MOUNTAIN CALLED

The Salish-speaking Cowlitz tribe were part of the Chinook
nation. They were among the Native Indians encountered
by the Lewis and Clark expedition in 1805. The Klickitat
tribe merged together with the Yakama tribe. Most
Klickitat descendants live on the Yakama and Grand Ronde
reservations today.

The mountain called St. Helens   in the Cascade Range
        was named for Baron St. Helens,
        British Ambassador to Spain.   Also considered Sa Kw
of the Lower Cowlitz   Lawetlat'la of Upper Cowlitz
        translated as "the smoker." What a thing, what a thing.

        No bottom, no top. I've also heard it called Loowit.

Volcanoes recall explosions, never statesmen.
        Sublime peak-a-boo.
Makes you wish you never held back
        your love.

Among Klickitat Indians an adolescent boy initiated
        into manhood
        ascended the slope. He'd sleep on the volcano's flank
                spirits hovering, filial.
        White naturalists, fur traders,
and painters gathered in exploring parties below.
        Sasquatch might visit. A glow appeared in the sky.

When I spotted the carved-out crater
                and log-jammed toxic lake

        I believed there could be fish with heads resembling bears.
And in the black stumps, standing dead Douglas firs I spy

my city's crumbling towers. No tantalizing lore.

Crisp morning disintegration   *9-11-01* MONTH/DAY/YEAR

Forever known for
enabling such euphemisms:

War on Terror

                Homeland Security   NSA Watch list

                        No Fly.

The mountain grows   back in geological time.

Towers rise in humanity's bang-em and build-em rhyme.

DUST LADY DIES OF CANCER

Marcy Borders, known as Dust Lady for the eerie photo
      That captured her covered in ash and grit

            after escaping   the South Tower on 9-11-01
            when she was 28
            a bank clerk, recently hired.

Exiting into a collapsing exoskeleton
            a photographer crouched down and clicked.

                  Her coat of grit blackened out the sun
            she waltzed into a wild storm

            a messenger.

            Couldn't sleep.
Lost her partner and   custody of her children.

Never discarded   the dusty dress
            One moment settled all others   like Miss Havisham.

            Only when Osama Bin Laden died could she stop drinking
Never afforded the medication   for her treatments.

Does dust ever wash off?

A coat of crime
Marcy died of cancer in August, 2015.

Remember her whole and happy   starting out

Immortal image of her affliction must enable insight

Not merely   evoke pity or fear.

HARRY TRUMAN OF ST. HELENS LODGE

Harry Truman, villain and pioneer.
    Crazy
     Wouldn't evacuate.

Cranky old fellow outlasted two wives
         Lived with sixteen cats.

He once saved Jack Nelson from drowning
in Spirit Lake. They lived on opposite sides of the water
         did not speak.

Harry arrived in 1925 and built Saint Helens Lodge
amid old Harmony Falls mine, logging roads,
        hobos like the Swede Ole.

      Harry drank with his guests and ran rum.
Originally from the hills of West Virginia
      His place sat amid clouds.

After earthquakes and venting eruptions of March, '80,
     huckleberry pickers and Ape Cave explorers,
       Read the sky, smelled the wind

Cowlitz Indians warned of venturing
        above timberline. "I'm staying," said
Harry. "Without me there's no story."

Karen Jacobsen, backcountry ranger
baked apple pie for Harry.
      "We didn't get to say goodbye."

His lodge disintegrated into tephra and ash

sank into the lake   Harry refused to blink

wearing airplane headphones to shush   belching fire.

MOUNTAIN WOMEN

—for Christine Colasurdo

They recruited women in the 1960s and '70s. To Harmony Falls,
Mt. Margaret, Spirit Lake. These rugged rangers hauled garbage,
enchanted tourists, bushwhacked trails. Sun-scorched, you
wouldn't call them hippies.
　　　They didn't dance　 to Kerouac and Burroughs.

After Pearl Harbor, women guarded supplies,
packed and rode horses. Helen, clerk-dispatcher, contacted Hazel
on Swift Lake, Carol on Coldwater. She monitored conditions,
and at night she read them comics
channeling Betty Boop over the line.

Mary Lou flew a seaplane to Spirit Lake after WWII and landed
at Harry Truman's dock. Her daughter fit inside the luggage rack.

Today, Christine fights global mining and logging clear-cuts.
Her family owned a cabin on Spirit Lake before the blast.
　　　She teaches calligraphy to adults,
　　　knows the names of every fern and flower.
　　　Directs my feet where to step.

Susan led the St. Helens Hiking Club.
Days before the volcano blew in 1980, she brought a group
to Minnie Lee's Mine
admiring Douglas firs and old Cedars
skirting
narrow cliffs
ringed with huckleberry.
One hiker counting steps mumbled
let's turn back.

In the end, Minnie Lee's Mine fell outside the blast zone.
Ash cloud cleared that narrow valley.

The Parker family, with a mother who recited so much lore
        she should have been a ranger
faced hurricane-force winds over 200 MPH.
Only their cabin floor remained   intact.

One of the bosses dared Helen and the girl lookouts
to visit Ole Peterson, bearded Van Winkle, Swedish hermit.
Tobacco and onions hung from his ceiling of hand-cut beams
he stirred a pot-bellied stove, surrounded by flowers and cobwebs.

The rangers sipped tea and stretched taut mountaineer legs
they wanted
        what they meant

Invincibility.

VOLCANO MOVES

The volcano moves like a man I know, crater dashed, puffing hot,
        riotous in ritual pride. Not only women wait to exhale.
Steamy insinuations . . . whatever resists eventually shifts.

A mountain is but a figment of your capacity
        shadow of your world maker
Registers a giant page of cloud in the misty Pacific Northwest
        Slowly clearing, holding you by your elbow.

Who were those people at the campground?
        They helped me blow up my Therma Rest pad, shared
           cranky cups of
Joe at 6 a.m. Conversation and hikes into the blast zone with its
    dead logs and
        razored honor. Scientists and writers, artists and idiots,
hours of disbelief, mesmerized by beauty gone gonzo.

        When we left the U-Fish Tower Rock campground
        We spread out across the country recalling
        stripes of snow and ash lining Saint Helens' flank.

A man I know moves me like a volcano
        how steamy, how stolid
he roars. Back hairy and warm
sudden motion overloads, predicting seismic activity
ashy rationalizations
        new flows and flowers
greater depth in mind and manifestation

        Yellow alert.

METALLIC THUD

—*for the Davids*

WORLD TRADE CENTER AND MOUNT ST. HELENS

"Step by step, breath by breath—no rush, no pain."
—*Gary Snyder*

1.

David Burns, insurance man   hears a metallic thud

just after morning coffee, September 11, 2001.

A crushing noise   a windy void.

He peers out his north-facing view

sees windows blown out eye level

only windows, no crater

shouts to anyone who will listen

shouts to the wind.

Some co-workers flee

to floor 78 express car

Liberty Street in a matter of seconds

before number two's crash.

2.

Column of steam, ash, rises 7,000 feet.

Ice and rock, wind a wild ride.

Cracks merge and become the "bulge."

Volcano souvenir business flourishes.

USGS scientist David Johnston measures the bulge on the north flank.

His observation point Coldwater II six miles northeast of St.
    Helens peak.

Sightseers press towards the steaming crater for closer view
    and photos.

3.

Bystanders and students watch as captives plummet from
    the towers,

missiles of grief. This is not television. Yes, it is.

"Go home," I shout. "Look away." Snails and stomachs and tails.

You know nothing of what's to come.

Dave Burns and his pal Paul rush onto the waiting Staten
    Island Ferry

engine ramps ramps ramps into the blue and black.

Life jackets all around in case of an aerial attack

It's not the engine, no, but a hulking dust cloud,

Time-made matter, a dirge.

4.

A 13,000-foot eruption of ash and steam

harmonic tremor signaling. Hot

seismic chart blot

May 12 a 5.0 earthquake underneath the north flank of St. Helens

triggers a small debris avalanche half a mile down.

Many people come out with cameras and binoculars.

Last chance for Spirit Lake landowners to evacuate.

5.

David Johnston perishes; David Burns survives.

Bones cut the wind.

More towers rise.

YETI IN PORTLAND

Yeti slinks through   the Pacific Northwest
> Out of the woods in the rain   he crosses the Willamette.

Wears a Columbia Gore-Tex pull over
> Rides a hybrid bike in all weather   but cannot become a
> vegan.

Knows caves and mud lahars
> Frolics in the tephra of early eruptions.

Munches on lupine. Knocks away standing dead and
> takes camouflage in organic debris.

No wonder his breath reeks.
He walks into the S.E. Portland bar as a lesbian folk trio
stands for their encore. Yeti needs a drink.

Wants to
make a
friend.

Loves Mt. Hood and St. Helens

He's a tall stranger also known as Big Foot,
Sasquatch
> mistaken for Chewbacca.

Someone asks him to remove his backpack. She looks like a poet.

He's claustrophobic and the applause hurts his ears.

Wants
beer
but
orders
a black Stumptown.

Yeti in the street   on eggshells wandering.

A mirror of forbidden shadows   between man and beast.

TWO

ASH FOR CASH

"Nature looks natural because it keeps
going, going, going like the undead . . . "

—Timothy Morton

DEAR GOVERNOR RAY

—for Lupita Lopez

Dixie Lee Ray, Washington state's first female governor,
    Served on the U.S. Atomic Energy commission
        appointed by Richard Nixon.

A Democrat, unmarried
      she gave herself a chain saw for Christmas.
           Gov. Ray wore sweat pants to a press conference
          Hired her sister as first lady
      Let a supertanker dock at Puget Sound.

On her watch, Mount St. Helens shocked the world in an
    election year
        On May 25, 1980   one week after the colossal eruption
      she declared   a red zone to keep away
           the unwary tourist and the thrill seeker.

Governor Ray went to FEMA
      begged for more money to pay for volcano disaster relief.

Citizens wrote to her, wrote to her, wrote to her, in ink and crayon.

Dear Governor: the air force should drop a bomb in that crater

      to loose it up and end all your troubles.

Governor do not use my tax money to pay for the rescue of
    the five men lifted

off Mount St. Helens after being told a number of times
          not to set foot in the area.

      Please send them a bill or make them go to jail.

Dear Governor Ray, my dearest lady, I am a prophet and
   visionary.

In my dream there is a station wagon with children in it
and the car stalls and the driver sees smoke and steam and lava.
   I will call at TV station and let them know.

         Dear Governor Ray: Let Russia Eat Our Dust!

VOLCANIC/PANIC

*"Many of them that sleep in the dust of the earth shall awake,
some to everlasting life, and some to shame and everlasting
contempt." [Dan. 12:2, KJV]*

1.

Poets and scientists struggle
to explain, to grasp
volcanology—a pyroclastic flow
is rapid
turbulent
hot gas undulating, escaping
fragments
ash
rock
lahar mudflow
fires flying in liquid
domes collapsing upon themselves.
We cannot stay away.

2.

"Private property"
cannot appease public needs.
The towers fell in fragments
scattered
beneath the rubble
spirits smoldering.

3.

Large tephra chunks of
Lapilli, (Italian, for the ash
Of Vesuvius).
Species return, some new to the
Cascade plain where forest had been.
We still live with the embers.
What about a simple memorial?
A national monument for all who pray or cry
Volcanic insides expose hot air.
Who may speak of rebuilding?
Light hits the pit where rubble lingers:
I hear something.

SIMON SAYS

The Twin Towers couldn't have collapsed like a pile of trash.
Disintegrating, vertically, swiftly, Simon says.
He accuses me of using the term conspiracy theory naively
    to dismiss views
that disagree with the official story.
        He believes that story is contrary to the laws of physics.

        Simon says it was an inside job. Bush needed a reason
    to go to war,
And Simon dismisses the influence of PTSD. I witnessed both
    planes
        hit and tried to ignore
        desperate workers dropping from the towers that
    afternoon
        evacuating students
from my campus, hushed, dismantling
        in deep dismay.

He says its pie-in-the-face obvious that the 9/11 report was a
    cover up.
        He writes in all caps:
        WE ARE NOT A GOOD MATCH.
A friend thought we might hit it off.

To other dating prospects, I write "we are not a match if you
    support Trump."
One man finds it heinous
        to pull out the rug from what hasn't even begun.
He sticks out forked tongue
And trolls me.

In these times
finding love: ice pick to brain,
Cold hard spike into the crevice of darkness.
        Politics cordoned off by fools who
write not so well, anger-soaked alt. arrows fly
        The other side of the other side.

Simon says, "place one hand
on my shoulder.
        Cover your mouth with the other."

ASH FOR CASH

Use ash to build   dikes along the rivers.
Make concrete   of pumice and sand.
Ash can be like pet rocks   new collectible.

Use horses instead of plows
          finger paint
          put ash in make-up.
Rub ash all over you   roll in it.

Rename Washington   Ashington.

If you place this stuff in a jar with the
          official state seal and a photo of Mount St. Helens
          you'd corner the market.

Too bad you can't   eat it.

In 1983 Crater House opened.
          The only retailer in the 110,000 acre
National Monument   six miles from
          Windy Ridge   serving
crater chicken   dome dogs
mountain burgers.

But farm workers   in the Yakima Valley
          can't breathe.

Wind, rain   fine particles
clog their noses and eyes.   Migrants lose
cash if they can't work   so they refuse

the doctor. They keep picking asparagus
          flecked with ash.

OWNERSHIP

Burlington Northern Railroad   once owned the crater
of Mount St. Helens volcano.
In 1982 the chairman and CEO wrote   to President Reagan

"We are pleased to advise you of our intention to donate our
ownership in the crater and the land adjoining Spirit Lake..."

Part of the checkerboard of public and private there's still
    land trading,
mining, cutting, collapsing. Beauty (but it's not cheap).

"We plant more than we cut," said the foreman.

The new tower   named "freedom,"
belongs to developers and feds. In exchange for the right to shop,
pay taxes, go to war, and remain flagrant targets. Where
    shall they keep remains?
        Spirits can't rest.

"We build more than we plant" said the foreman.

The first surges rushed down   the volcano's
    northern flank at 80 mph
Smith Creek, Pine Creek, Muddy River   the South Fork of
    the Toutle River.
        Mud lahars buried cars, mailboxes, farms, roads.

Destroyed 16 bridges 1100 miles of state roads closed.
Old growth Douglas fir, western red cedar western hemlock
and noble fir ascended   2000 feet above the lake
        eradicated quickly.

They found bones   a few blocks from the Twin Towers
more than 10 years after the attack. Between the cracks as
    they demolished old scaffolding
for multimillion-dollar condos   they excavated a skull, a tibia
what might have been a jaw.   Whose brother or mother?

Concern floats for a millisecond whispers between lovers'
    despair.

"You mourn, we own," said the foreman.

BLIND SPOT

—for Fred Swanson

Never mended my blind spot—thought the volcano moved.
    A graphic novel monster, stationary molten rock.

At Windy Ridge, Mt. St. Helens, 30 years post-eruption
    appears close, cartoon-like, cracked.

Cell phone powers up approaching the ridge—four bars.
    A series of beeps in your pocket.
Imagine those hikers falling off a snow cornice
    thinking they stood on solid rock, not packed snow.
Posing for a photo, they slid down the south face
    blurred in winter's muted light, flashes of old growth
    charred in pyroclastic flow.

No more solid than the peak that once glistened distant
    On blue Portland days.

What you can't fathom finds you.

Objects unto obliteration.

LOSSES WE COVER

—for Elaine Equi

We will pay for
Damage to the property for direct loss
By volcanic eruption
Including volcanic blast
Shock wave, lava flow
And volcanic fallout
We do not cover loss to
Trees, shrubs, lawns, and grounds
Harmed directly or
indirectly
By earthquake, landslide, mud flow
Tidal wave, flooding or earth
sinking, rising, or shifting
One or more volcanic eruption
Shall constitute a single eruption.

The deductible
provisions of this policy
Apply to this coverage of

Treatment is available
for those who worked
in the rescue, recovery or clean up

Survivors who lived, worked or went to school
the NYC Disaster area
are eligible
if you know someone you think might benefit
from the WTC Health program
encourage them to contact us

Were you there? Was someone you know there?
Within a 72-hour period
Your words might help them get care.

Practitioners provide high quality mental health
and provide treatment for cancers
Additional cancers will be added to the list of

LOSSES WE COVER.

SMOKE

Smoke alights. Sinister plume

angled by the wind
        off the towers before they crumbled

It could go this way or that...Brooklyn, Jersey, uptown

underground any town my town.

        Into Canada a hole in the sky.

Between your eyelashes touching silk.

        Defiling plants and water

reaches into mother's milk

Tooth and nostril

the world's outer inner line.

Black smoke of a thousand chemical drifts.

White smoke of annihilation.

Red smoke of pained regeneration.

Blue smoke of ocean crest.

True bleeding in the marsh of landfill

Smoke in a blanket of rain.

FALL TO PIECES

—for Gary Snyder

The Cowlitz tribe called it Lawetlat'la, or Smoking Mountain.
    They were not fooled by the stunning snow-covered
  peak
casting perfect reflection into   a glass blue lake.
    A wondrous spirit scooped up the earth and created
  Mt. Rainier.
Then formed Smoking Mountain and Mt. Adams too
    the jealous husband of quarreling wives.

Fire, rocks, hot molten ash--one of the wives had her head
  knocked off.
    Spokane Indians in 1839 told a missionary that an
  eruption bored
      holes   in the earth and tore trees and elk to pieces.

Before the white man came, Chief Bighead had a dream.
    Thunder overhead and people crying in terror.
      Dry snow came to dance.

"Soon from the rising sun will come a different kind of man
    from any you have ever seen. He will bring a book
  and teach from it.
Afterwards the world will
    fall to pieces."

Before David A. Johnston died
      he collected volcanic gas samples from a
  fumarole high on
    the unstable northern side of St. Helens.

He was among the first to see the May 18 eruption
    and sent a warning to control center
      the black billowing front of the lateral blast
outpacing his legs.

They found his gear and his camera
developed his witness film   20 years later.

THREE

OFF-SIDE

—for my neighbors and my son, Joshua

OFF-SIDE

—for Joshua Fish

Prepared for rain, we arrive early wearing ponchos.
Search for soccer field number two, Red Hook, Brooklyn
In striking distance of Ikea's flagship,
Stockholm-on-the-Gowanus.
Blackened factories, ships' containers
Trucks fire up tacos, serve plantains and guava drinks.

Our team gets called off-side
Again, and again, a whistle, a hand, nothing counts.
A foot might wedge or pivot in air
And end up east or west, anywhere.
We don't stand a chance against the bulky Latinx strikers
elbows gnash their bony-boy physiques
in fancy uniforms, shiny red-and-yellow cleats.
Our coach's panicky indignation fails to ignite passion
The ball arrives first.

The others barrel it into our net when we miss.
Their siblings' mock-kick on the sidelines.
A dog runs on the field.

Losing takes grace.
I head to the truck for a shake
Amid whistles, bewilderment
One boy boots a crushed Pepsi can
Into the blinding sun.

LOST FRIENDS

I lost the friend who tells me I should not hit "reply all" and that I should "scroll down." I lost the one who scolds me for my tip in the Mexican restaurant to the friend who says you can't eat fish in my presence. The one with whom you can't discuss sex, but you can discuss money.

The close friend who maintains a separate apartment from her husband now goes bike riding early mornings with my friend who retired early. They watch birds and eat breakfast.

On the terrace after my birthday dinner, the boyfriend of my friend who attends Mets games with me talked only to the husband of the friend I hardly see because she buys clothes for her grown children and claims obligations every Shabbat. The boyfriend feels uncomfortable listening to women talk about their writing, but he cannot escape sandwiched in the corner. Until his girlfriend gives him the nod to worm away.

I lost friends to their partners and kids, lost friends in France and Italy to circumstance, or was it something I said? My former college roommate became a Trump apologist. I lost another friend to an early death. Looking at an old telephone book filled with names and numbers. Bygone days and nights, quiet forgetting. No, not really.

MOM OUT OF THE BLEACHERS

—for Kendra

A pitched ball hits a boy in the face, 60 or 70 mph.
He's beaned in the chin   blood drips fast on his
    Braves uniform.
Game delayed.   Game on.

From out of the bleachers   one mom trails us.
She wipes his forehead   with a wet towel
    I fill out forms
    In the private, nearby emergency room.

This blonde mom   whom I had labeled aloof
knows when to stay and when to go.

        My child is lucky.
He only needs stitches that darken his chin like a goatee
        he may grow someday.

He had only known injury   as abstract as a Jackson Pollack.
        Let's witness the opposition fall to pieces   he says,
    anxious.

The blonde mom holds his hand.

I talk to the doctor, calm.
Frisson of the fields, dryness in our throat

What assurance covers
Insurance won't.

DAYCARE DADS

Their husbands have crinkled skin around the eyes.
Wear their babies, talk with British or regional Americas
    accents.
Sweaters over jeans, they work hard—tight combination
of sunset and wind.

I wanted a turn on the carousel.
Hand-carved horses playful and domesticated.
Old world style seeking modern entitlement.
Ride might get scary high or ludicrously low.
The wives walk past.

Don't know what's it like to live with these guys, or if they
    change the nappies.
Strong hands button little coats. They aren't young, these
    well-worn urban-rugged daddy men,
lifting up babes like bountiful packages.

Some have joint custody, their anger a small cut left
    untended, possibly infected.
Some have the look of a sand blasted scaffold, holding up a
    structural castle.

Could I please unwrap one, please? I won't wreck him. A fine-
    tuned time-ripened mellow master
in a jeep, balding or salt and pepper.

Needing less drink, more sleep
        I'm waiting by the cubicle, off the hook

        swinging a small coat.

I NEVER HAD A DAUGHTER

I never had a daughter
who play-acted feelings
     she could not articulate
     dolls in hand.
Who wrote poems and   scored goals.
     Who asked, "mother who was your first love?
Who was your third?"

I never had a daughter who
     flipped   long hair
Sitting outside   texting among six friends
     Spooning ice cream into their firm, fool mouths.
One friend spoke too frankly   my girl cried.
Then she blindsided
     every try. Every tale of recounting
        her mother's   odd ordeals.

I never had a daughter
     of charm or dismay
     Rebellious   clingy
After snapping and snarling
     She'd hug me round the knees.

To have raised   a child on one's own
  a fever pitch of   errors and trials begun at age 40.
     So, my son   he never had
     A sister.

STAND CLEAR OF THE CLOSING DOORS

If there's loss take to the real
Home is a bone-deep breath.

Windswept sounds of where
It's the people before time.

Their voices touch you in the morning
Alone blue flying, the crime of trying.

Make more. Sleeping notion.
Hand in face instead of bed.

Focus soft cut.
End open.

Before the time where
bone people

fly.   Blue   soft crimes.
Try to sleep. Face in the morning

Windswept breath.
Stand clear of the closing doors.

NEWARK

—for Joel Lewis

Who will be supported by these rust-colored beams?
        Ironworkers scratch in their names—Local #11
We will be tall, obscured in fiberglass.
        Miles above integrated turnpikes and industrial parks.

I missed the cherry blossoms in Branch Brook Park,
        couldn't find Ferry Street.
Looked up, walked past.

There's Muzak on the Jersey Transit platforms
        An old lady staggers
        drunk or sick of time.

Watching crowds   come off the escalator.
On a Saturday afternoon   beyond the approach
of narrow platform.   People fall asleep and wake
        in the light of that eye.

She will pull in past the middle rail
        When the doors part and speed us away

From the blurring outlines of a city's new sweep

        Electrical, rhetorical

already spoken for.

SHARK WEEK

I don't know you. We may never meet.
Virtual image and messages typecast.
Imagine a space or a face, word gorge
flying past regular stages
       Living in code gore, body parts fly.
                In-person spontaneity dies.

Can't say I like it. How many ways
To be estranged?   Apps figure
your taste in music; games distract you
       from reading books.

       Ads follow you like fox hunters
Waiting to bag and skin.
       Men on screens scream
They post shots of glittering motorcycles while shirtless.
       Children pop out of their hats.

One can lower oneself into the sea.
       Be brave and calm

Thank heavens "Shark Week"
       Has come and gone.

       It's always Shark Week.

SWEEP-SECOND HAND

Fingering a token
A tie-up on the Major Deegan road
Thoughts race ahead of thoughts
Interrupting feet
A molecular passing
Through Marvin Gaye's
Grapevine.

DREAM OF THE MAN
WHO WRITES STREET POEMS

—*for John Godfrey*

I become numb feet in snow. Streets recede,
Never noticed how slow cars roll.

To keep warm, streetwalkers make soliloquies
Rushing, I read you—meeting her.

Wish my street sense was enormously appearing
As you busted in snow covered
to find danger as lovely.

Dig out your drill heart: meet me fate.

ABECEDARIAN: SHE CRIES

At the drop of a hat, she cries.
Because of winter's gradual
Consistent rain soaking her
Down jacket. She cries at times
Even in her white mask.
For the wind's fury as much as for fear of COVID.
Gradually tears drip down to her hand.
Held sometimes by one person, in fingerless gloves.
In fact, they walk together while it pelts them.
Just like in Rhianna's anthem "Under my Umbrella."
Kaleidoscopic tears with sheen as days
Loom lighter. She gets stopped
More than before when she was ignored.
Not for nothing, for curiosity's sake.
Often Gen Z or Millennials
Point. "Look at how she's sobbing."
Question for you, Mam—can we help you feel better?
Really though, can't a person cry for the pure
Sensation? Considering cosmic vicissitudes?
Three years of pandemic, isolation, upheavals.
Underwhelming or overwhelming city life?
Various monuments and shops gone.
Why even a place like Bed Bath & Beyond,
Xanadu for kitchenware, bedding, and candy too.
Yesterday's wandering brought wise tears.
Zealous emotions. Open, everywhere.

FUNDRAISER FOR HACKENSACK RIVER KEEPER

The venue: Redd's Bar in Carlstadt by Met Life Stadium.
Self-proclaimed "Times Square of New Jersey,"
hosts a fundraiser for Hackensack River Keeper.
That "S" curve of a waterway welcomes 125 species of birds
despite Jersey's vast industrial immolation.

Brant
Mute Swan
Wood Duck
Gadwall
Mallard

Volunteers arrest garbage.
Guided paddles go at low and high tide
Cherry berry tones in Redd's Cabernet.
Jackie Mason's daughter takes the stage
talking shit and stereotyping.

Make it funny. Make it last.

Blue-winged Teal
Northern Shoveler
Double-crested Cormorant

Near dark smokestacks
Jackie's daughter screeches.

Great Blue Heron
Yellow-crowned Night Heron
Ruddy Duck

We'll keep paddling—no more fiddle faddle:
rectify the meadow, renew the land.

FLY AND RAPPEL

—homage to Elizabeth Streb, founder of S.L.A.M.
(Streb Lab for Action Mechanics)

Dancers held slack in "jerk vests"   attached to cables
on their backs.
Diva Streb orchestrates from the sidelines as her
black Spandex team pulls ropes   attached to pulleys.
They heave like ancient builders, muscles and magicianship.
          They yank and recoil so
          aerial faeries can fly

Open rehearsals in Williamsburg, Brooklyn: think of bridges
          think of death
                    everyone's welcome inside the hangar.

Dance at "100 mile per hour."
Streb knows real moves happen   in unconventional

SPACE.

BODIES agree to fly   and   fall

          LIFTED and
THREATENED

Using cable and flight, building blocks of cinema
          Synchronized eyes field vertical drops.

You get jerked and fall, FREE.
Artistic velocity: gorgeous air vamps

Sweat, contradiction   across
                    the ramps of time.

JOE'S PIZZA HEARTBREAK SLICE

Joe's pizza slice a ruckus
        of eat me now
drenched in liquid cheese

knees pressed against other knees

how you came to me   at first
        sliced off   the rest
        I'm
        dripping
love a messy inconvenience
        Fussy pie-shaped lie

Pizza gooey good
eat it alone   standing with strangers

thought bubbles clog
the present tense
doughy crust
crushed pepper
        burning

grease, moist eyes, heat

Have to have another.

PLAYINGSTYLE

Is pregnancy   queer?
Does it have anything to do   with an overheard phone
Conversation   the pregnant girl's walking talk
Kurt Vile's guitar playingstyle   pleased
the bartender so much she shifted steam.
Capo, open tuning   hammer on the neck
A patron asked her   to put salt on the winter ice
outside the Spotty Dog bar where cigarette smokers
linger. Is privilege an accusation or a happening stance?
He played banjo
then guitar   with reverb.
I was pregnant   while old   nothing shaped like the
Belly-button-bulging girl's   walking talk
Touched by your lack of   aversion to "they"
A person's personal pronoun   is a choice
A playingstyle   so magnanimous. Free We.

BEND

Listen they say. Listen better. Listen more.
You know all the passwords to his accounts
        Not to him.
He's teeming with philosophy
beneath a veneer of calm.
Wears his headphones at all times
But doesn't hear you even
when
        they're off.

He's a trickster heralding his animal
Non-verbal yet brisk in his corner
        on the rise.
With a magnetism that flows
        When away from home.

He communicates on his terms
And walks away freely
What is force? What is love?
What he doesn't realize he cannot
        bend.

FOUR

POST-TRAUMATIC POSTS

" . . . we returned to a place of wild devastation . . . "
—STEPHANIE IZAREK AND DAN COSTA

CAVE EXPLORERS REQUEST PERMISSION
TO ENTER THE RED ZONE

We are snails.   You know our shells.

    William R. Halliday, Seattle thoracic surgeon, Navy
veteran.
    Explores caves from Okinawa to Zanzibar,
British Columbia to Yucatan.

Treads within treads
    writes everything down.

The afternoon dankness inside   the dream beyond death.

Speleologists request permission   to enter the RED ZONE.
    Excavate tubes   depths within depths.

We bore into openings where the first explorers claimed
    Ape men threw rocks.
    We scuttle and breathe the remnants.

Governor Ray, DO NOT DENY US ACCESS.

Eleven loggers perished, but they are cutting   they
    are felling.

We measure ash.
Leave behind equipment and warm waterproof clothing
    in the event of another eruption.

We are bears who never hibernate.
Call us cave guests, known as Trogloxenes.

In Ape Cave, the longest lava tube cave   in the
    continental U.S.

A wedge-shaped area south of St. Helens and Mount Adams
    Formed in late Pleistocene and in recent time.

We crave crystalline.
Outside, fresh growth on conifers
Elk tracks elegant.

We enter openings, porous hands. We're almost home.

SAFE (UNTRUE)

—*for Kimberly Flynn*

In my eye's mind
     the red zone burned
as a pit, as a pile

     Do-gooders passed buckets
         Amid skeletal remains and chunks of steel.

We smelled its glow
       Sensed   dense hope

Politicians   craved revenge
     We breathed   suspicion

     In our eye's mind
neighbors ready, real
       back to work   back to school
       they claimed   ALL SAFE ALL SOUND.

In my mind's mind
     we could bake casseroles for hook-and-ladder crews

     But the bathtub we soaked in submerged our skin

embers in a barge.

Who got sick? Who flew?

Eyes and minds and years of hell

     Proved safe

Already always misstated (UNTRUE).

AERIAL

It's a fiction to depict administrative
approval as a wooing.

Deem me up.

Impossible skeletal
deportment

an American in limbo at the airport.

Time zones as cloud cover
either side of continental divide.

From 33,000 feet you cannot tell

this is a racist nation.

O'Hare a rainy field of maximums.

Starbucks coffee on the brain.

You feel yourself evaporating
into gridlock caused by Fidel
Castro's UN appearance.

Airspace bus train subway
unfocused landing

in familiar home pockets: water main breaks.

DISASTER TOURISM
(AFTER SUPER-STORM SANDY)

Gape at water rising on your street   crossing a barricade
And a park   cascading past a highway.

Cobblestone not quaint in a flood   WATER RUSHES

          into subway stations caressing Zuccotti Park,
foaming at the mouth.

Where
they removed the occupiers one by one. Peeled them from
benches   kicked in tents.

Water wastes no words
          expunges urges
                    humans' recoil.

Our wired world silenced.

          Electricity mute in darkness

blown circuits wet interchanges   fingers in sockets.

          cell phones   inert

Low-lying luxury homes upended

          Amusement parks reduced to distended parts
                    Ferris wheel submerged in seaweed.

Cars, legs, planks, pathos

gaping politicos

Who can we call?

Homes and honesty affronted
Encroaching jiggy jiggy boom boom.

      Like tourists we line up,
but
won't change our currency.

We don't protect the mother of all mothers.

Surprise ingested   like medical marijuana.

      Bite your tongue.   Wait it out.   Pray.

Change must be a full-time affair   not when we decide to stop
    texting

      Run to anti-apocalypse   the sustainable
    remaining extinction rebellions

Of Time.

SOME ORDINARY GODDESSES

—for Marjorie

Krishna played his flute and drove the Gopis wild;
He pleasured each one differently.
To be insatiable—a curse, but one feels that way.

Hard to stay still, accept less as more, a one-person exhibit as
    it were.

Krishna served each cowherd girl by multiplying—
A deity who tends to affairs of state,
Non-possessive, with musical genius.

Some ordinary goddesses eat grapes and cheese,
swim in rivers and quarries.
They fit into lotus petals and float, heeding the calls of their
flocks.

These days a semi-Krishna's blue ass should succumb
to the full moon's sagacity.

Spread pleasure through rife fields
Bleating sheep, keep repeating

Krishna—dash the trampled monoculture

    Of our Western hearts.

CODA: "LAYLA"
BY DEREK AND THE DOMINOES

The second part of "Layla" before the bird sings, the famous Coda
Makes you wish you rode on a swing.
Your legs
pump hard   and high.

Duane Allman's slide guitar   sells it
refrain overrides desire   piano contains
a singer's blood.
        Another man's wife   nostalgic filaments.

Listening to "Layla" we don't know to know
        melody sans words   cling to us.
Cease to pump,
        coast for a while.
Resonant being   in wind and rain.
        Ask for that rush and stroke.

The riff   was lifted by the drummer
        from his ex-wife   later he became a delusional killer.

We're overwrought
        by remarkable lushness   piano and slide
                Flock to its   wistful heaven.

BLANKS (ICELAND 5)

What can I say about those who leave behind no books?
My father kept no journals.
No collection of letters or the latest in technological
    communiques.
No reflections, or artwork. Only photos, a few collectibles
like
stamps and coins. His World War II medal of honor that
came
many, many years after the war. His investments live on as benefits.
Friends and family know of his stories, but those peers are
gone.
Cultures leave
behind origin tales even if we don't know who wrote them,
like Icelandic sagas,
African griot songs. Some get written. Others gnaw at bones
    in the ground.

My son is not certain he will read what I write.
That record of spark and sprawl.
Old time magic in the region of my mind.
He has taken little interest in the missing side of his origins.

Some of us will leave behind books in boxes, giant piles on
shelves
Moving on with what strange holes
In the world.

SUCCESSION

If a forest is cleared by lava, charred and burned down

one species is replaced, others lost.

Resurgence?
Extinction?
Blur of blade?

What sprout gains clout when it had none?

Lava felled a forest at Mount St. Helens. Pyroclastic plain enabled
      a mole.
Purple Lupine would have choked without sun
      It begins blooming. Soil bequeaths its
      impetus, elements change.

Humans? Evolution
      of pollution.

Logging interests and mines disrupt

the chain. Property and gunpowder.

Those in power want to frack our backs for gas
Drill for ore. Cut us up and smoke us.
Blow us up through our assholes.

Time needs time   maps be glades before drawings drew

Sun filters. Close the spigot.

Console me modern drain pipe. *Turn to Seed.*

POST-TRAUMATIC POSTERS

—for Jim Conley

We hid in your apartment   with our two-year olds

On the border of evacuation and underground.

No waterfalls and tourists. You said we should stay

there with Legos and hula hoops. Not go anywhere.

Invisible judgments   and footprints

TV and soundtrack outside   sirens and blasts

The bathtub   where toddlers soak

in blissful ignorance of terrorism,

mangled feet and furniture fragments.

Tribeca trifecta calculations

post-traumatic poster children   know their

parents are gone

or they know nothing.

Now, a 9-11 Museum and shopping, a transit hub.

Selfies on the plaza

And the shiny briny steel tower and hulking Oculus.

First responders   facing death

Can't get health benefits from D.C.

The slurry wall leaked like their intestines.

You and I barely listened

Watching the toddlers lope

Post madness, mirth.

While all the ladders and engines and heroes

        took care of whomever they could

We saved each other. Now we rarely speak.

        I hope I mean more   to you

Then that fast hug   on the street

        That public-relations gaze.

I never knew   you   and you

        Grasp little   of me.

Grown-up make substitutes: Night for day and day for disarray.

        Not like our children   playing
        We count ourselves awake.

        Witnesses. Is that enough?

NIGHT LIGHT

Stay awake. Look beyond
clock chimes   how quiet
and sensible the warm, heated room
and trumpet life extols all sources.

Legs of table settle your arrangements
the night light of roaming
in your room.

At that hour
a passage of greetings
from another glossary.

You pick up a book
as protection from
rambling.

Mirror of consciousness
in river's dark presence
beyond the brick walls
of high-rise housing.

Stay awake. Objects
and words first, later dreams

of gambling
and winning on the

number "six."

ALL THE ASH

All the ash of my life smudges the margins of this page
        ashes fleck my radio mind.

With surprises of great and fallow tunes
It is that or this?
        The comic, the classic, the getaway
Near and just missing a mark.

Ash of dark dreams with bright white lines
Does that mean you can always escape?
        Might you
toss and turn into   discord?

Ash on my forehead, ash in my shirt
Am I a token statistic, or burned up tree?

By the seat of the sea
By the ribbon of the climate
By the relief of those escaped
Of those that want to go backwards, break us down.
Build and build and build till there's no light
With ash we paint a redolent world.

We exhale. We plant.
Carve with breathtaking

Hindsight.

GRAPPLE

—for Mark and Jackie Margolis

Piece of steel from the South Tower
floors 30-33
       folded over unto itself.

Like a bendy branch
       a kneeling knee
three or four welds split open.

My son walks ahead of me
       as we the elders survey these artifacts
       we don't want to remember that day
       he's anxious to review the main events.

He was only two back then.
Fifteen years after the attack
I cannot enter the recap room.
       My lungs contain tiny particles.

       He explores
photos of carnage and smoke
parts of firetrucks and teddy bear mountains
posters of missing souls and recordings about heroes.

       He lives without questioning behemoths
built after terror trembles. Inside the museum the
dead and alive
       form
       a column of
       voices.

We all grapple with
       distance and proximity

Reprise:

    Drum
    Drum
    Drum

    the island

    the river

    the sky

    always with us

    after

    all

    other

    signs.

CHANCE PLAYED A ROLE

Chance   played a role   in rebuilding

     biological communities.

Patches of alders   clumps of sedges   fireweed

creatures   made their way in new habitats

after 14-miles of ash

and snow induced mud-flow

erosion   made desert-like   soil.

Survivors, like those who fled the twin towers safely, or
who never went to work that day.
Saplings and shrubs buried in spring snow lived through
the blast that killed taller trees.

Hangers-on, created a new legacy rich in nitrogen   and
    carbon.

Traveling salamanders did well in gopher tunnels.

Red-legged frogs endangered elsewhere, thrive at St. Helens.

Human-induced climate change   not like a volcano

The Hudson River, hugging lower Manhattan in a flood zone.

Towers blockade the sky in our windows.

Humans meander among machines, dreaming of messengers
    in the shape of animals and stars.

CHERYL J. FISH published her debut novel *Off the Yoga Mat*, in 2022, and in 2021, her collection of poems, *The Sauna is Full of Maids*, celebrating Finnish sauna culture, friendship, and travel, came out from Shanti Arts. Fish's poems have appeared in *Hanging Loose*, *Maintenant*, *Terrain*, *Mom Egg Review*, *New American Writing*, *Reed*, *Postcard poems*, *Volt*, *Santa Monica Review*, *About Place Journal*, *ISLE*, and *Poetics for the More-than-Human-World*. Fish's short fiction has appeared in *Cheap Pop*, *Iron Horse*, *Liars League*, *Spank the Carp*, *Boog City*, *Gargoyle*, *Apricity*, and *KGB BarLit*. She was nominated for a 2024 Pushcart Prize and is a creative writing editor at the journal *Ecocene: Cappadocia Journal of Environmental Humanities*. She co-curates a reading series, VillageStorySalon, at The New York Public Library and teaches workshops online and in person for Art in the Basin, The Queens Public Library, The San Miguel Writers Conference, and elsewhere. Her website is cheryljfish.com.

www.ingramcontent.com/pod-product-compliance
Lightning Source LLC
Chambersburg PA
CBHW031145090426
42738CB00008B/1225